EARLY ONE AFTERNOON in the mid-1990s, a then-colleague of mine, Judge John Sprizzo of the U.S. District Court for the Southern District of New York, and I were returning from lunch, and as we walked up Pearl Street in lower Manhattan, he surveyed the scene – a dump truck blocking vehicular access to the street; concrete barriers in front of the courthouse; deputy U.S. marshals brought in from other districts around the country, clad in black SWAT uniforms and bulletproof vests, carrying firearms of a sort more associated with the battlefield than the cityscape. Sprizzo shook his head: "What the hell are we doing here? This is a military problem, not a legal problem." That casual comment has seemed, at least in retrospect, like lightning in the middle of the night, suddenly and starkly illuminating the landscape before darkness envelops it again. Of course, even the darkest night gives way to dawn, and it should by now be clear to all but the most obtuse that terrorism is substantially a military problem, and military means and measures, even military

tribunals, are the appropriate way to deal with some or all of it.

The scene Judge Sprizzo was looking at and reacting to had been precipitated by the February 1993 bombing of the World Trade

---

It should by now be clear to all but the most obtuse that terrorism is substantially a military problem, and military means and measures, even military tribunals, are the appropriate way to deal with some or all of it.

Center that killed six people; injured more than a thousand and caused tens of millions of dollars in damage; and led to the trial of four of the perpetrators. Among the plotters' announced goals was securing freedom for El Sayyid Nosair, who had been convicted in the state courts of New York in connection with the November 1990 murder of Meir Kahane, a right-wing Israeli politician shot by Nosair just after delivering a speech in a midtown New York hotel. Oddly, the prosecutors had presented so many overlapping witnesses with contradictory accounts of the shooting that Nosair was actually acquitted of the murder but convicted of using the weapon involved. At the time he committed his crime, Nosair had been dismissed as a lone misfit. The contents of his apartment, including jihadist literature and writings containing fantasies about attacking the United States by toppling tall buildings, had sat largely unexamined in a warehouse until after the 1993 bombing. Indeed, an amateur video of Kahane's November 1990 speech, examined in 1993, would show that present in the hall, in addition to Nosair, was Mohammed Salameh, who would later participate in the 1993 bombing to help free Nosair. Other evidence would show that Nosair was supposed to have made his escape by getting into a cab driven by Mahmud

Abouhalima, another 1993 bomber, and was captured when he jumped into the wrong cab and eventually had to flee on foot.

There would be later plots, successful and unsuccessful. A partial list includes the plot in December 1994 and January 1995 to blow up airliners over the Pacific, which actually resulted in one bombing in December 1994 that killed a Japanese engineer on a flight from the Philippines to Tokyo. In addition, there were the 1998 car bombings, moments apart, at the U.S. Embassies in Nairobi, Kenya, and Dar es Salaam, Tanzania, that killed 224 people and wounded thousands, and the millennium plots that included a plan to blow up Los Angeles International Airport, foiled when Ahmed Ressam, betrayed by his nervous demeanor, was captured aboard a Seattle ferry with a bottle of explosives in the trunk of his car. An attempt to blow up the destroyer USS *The Sullivans* in Aden, Yemen, failed when the would-be suicide bombers overloaded their skiff with explosives and it sank. The follow-up of that attack, in October 2000, was the bombing of the USS *Cole* in Aden, Yemen, which killed 17 sailors.

And there would be other trials, including the trial of Ramzi Yousef, mastermind of the 1993 World Trade Center bombing and architect of the Pacific airliner bombings. There was also the trial of Omar Abdel Rahman, the so-called "blind sheikh," and several codefendants, including Nosair, for a wide-ranging terrorist plot that encompassed the Kahane murder in 1990; the 1993 World Trade Center bombing; and a plan to blow up various critical sites in New York City, including the Lincoln and Holland tunnels, FBI headquarters in Manhattan, and the United Nations. Finally, there was the prosecution of millennium bomber Ahmed Ressam.

The 1993 World Trade Center bombing was described at the time as a wake-up call to this country to take notice that it was dealing with something broader than random criminal acts. That something was Islamic violence to which this country was no longer immune. Unfortunately, our response to each subsequent act was framed in the argot of conventional criminal prosecution: a stern declaration that we would "bring to justice" those responsible. The ongoing assumption was that "justice" meant a trial in a federal court, with attendant discovery for the defendants and their supporters outside the courtroom of not only the evidence the government would introduce to convict them but also of some of the means and methods used to gather that evidence. This presented a trove of intelligence for those on the outside. For example, when the government followed the standard practice in conspiracy cases of disclosing to the defense the unindicted conspirators in the prosecution of Omar Abdel Rahman, the "blind sheikh," the list included Osama bin Laden; it was learned years later that that list found its way within weeks to bin Laden in Khartoum, Sudan.

Perhaps not unnoticed during all of this, but certainly not taken at face value, was the declaration by Osama bin Laden, first published in a London newspaper in August 1996 and reissued in 1998, that included a call to "every Muslim who believes in God and wishes to be rewarded to comply with God's order to kill the Americans and plunder their money wherever and whenever they find it."

After September 11, 2001, the Bush administration made it clear that conventional criminal investigation and prosecution would no longer set the limit of the government's response. Although few had taken bin Laden seriously when he issued his call in 1998, September 11 seemed to mark a turning point. To "bring them to justice" was added "bring justice to them." Relying on the Authorization for Use of Military Force issued by Congress in the days following the terrorist attacks, the administration went to war. That disconcerted many, not only those on the left, who may be expected to cringe at any assertion of executive power, particularly by a Republican administration, but even those actually engaged in the business at hand. Thus, for example, Islamic fundamentalism was not identified as the source of the problem. Indeed, even as he mobilized the nation in an address to Congress, President Bush assured us that Islam is a religion of peace and said that it had essentially been kidnapped by a band of extremists. To savor how far political correctness has carried us, and in what direction, imagine President Roosevelt telling Congress on December 8, 1941, that the peaceful Shinto religion had been kidnapped by a cabal of militarists. The Bush administration presented the war as "a war on terrorism." Anyone with a pulse knew who was supposed to be in the crosshairs. But "global war on terrorism" did not invite precise analysis of either the nature of the threat or who presented it. On the contrary, it gave an opening to those who opposed the whole enterprise. Some carped at imagined hypocrisy because the effort was directed only at Muslims and not at the IRA, Basque separatists, Peru's Shining Path guerrillas, etc. Others claimed derisively that it was at least misleading to speak of a war against a tactic rather than those employing it or their goal.

Like many disputes that engage the attention of lawyers (and the controversy over our response to terrorism has engaged lawyers to a degree never before seen in our history), this dispute turned as much heated attention on the label as on what was inside the package. The choice of label, it appeared, would determine the outcome of the debate. This was particularly so in a conflict in which the adversary did not follow the rules of war and should not have been able to invoke the protections of those rules. If the struggle legitimately could be called a war, then all the powers available to fight a war, including everything from intelligence gathering to detention of captured combatants, would be available to us. Also, because our adversaries did not accept international conventions that had been put in place to try to civilize war to the extent possible – wearing uniforms, carrying arms openly, following a recognized chain of command, not targeting civilians – they could not reasonably invoke the protection of those conventions.

Despite its recourse to euphemism ("religion of peace," etc.), the Bush administration responded to 9/11 with a clear-eyed recognition that going to war was a difficult choice, fraught with difficult consequences, including difficult legal consequences. As long as the Bush administration remained in office, the legal norms of a struggle called "war" would prevail. For a good part of the period between September 2001 and January 2009, when the Obama administration assumed control of the executive branch, Congress gave at least grudging assent. The 2001 Authorization for Use of Military Force was followed by the USA Patriot Act. This authorized, for the investigation of terrorism, surveillance techniques and other measures that had been used before in conventional criminal investigations.

The involvement of the nation's courts in issues underlying this war, specifically the federal courts led by the Supreme Court, has been, to use a term dear to President Obama, unprecedented. Opponents of the Vietnam War tried to take to the courts in an effort to stop it, but they failed. Opponents of the government's tactics against terrorism have had far more success. One prisoner held at the U.S. military base at Guantanamo Bay succeeded in challenging the government's right to charge him before a military commission without congressional authorization. Congress responded with the necessary approval in the Military Commissions Act of 2006. But the Supreme Court would be receptive as well to the rights of detainees, even outside the United States at Guantanamo Bay, to challenge the lawfulness of their detention by requiring their jailer to meet the standards applicable to civilian prisoners exercising the historic right to petition by habeas corpus.

It was not always thus. During World War II, the United States held hundreds of thousands of German and Italian prisoners of war – the vast majority of whom fought in strict obedience to the laws of war, and tens of thousands of whom were confined at camps in the United States mainland – without even one of them being permitted to challenge his confinement by filing a habeas corpus petition in a federal court. In *Johnson v. Eisentrager*, an opinion handed down after the end of World War II, Robert Jackson, who served not only as attorney general and then as a Supreme Court justice, but also as this nation's chief prosecutor at Nuremberg, derided the very idea that a prisoner of war could petition for a writ of habeas corpus:

> *The writ, since it is held to be a matter of right, would be equally available to enemies during active hostilities as in the present twilight between war and peace. Such trials would hamper the war effort and bring aid and comfort to the enemy. They would diminish the prestige of our commanders, not only with enemies but with wavering neutrals. It would be difficult to devise more effective fettering of a field commander than to allow the very enemies he is ordered to reduce to submission to call him to account in his own civil courts and divert his efforts and attention from the military offensive abroad to the legal defensive at home. Nor is it unlikely that the result of such enemy litigiousness would be a conflict between*

judicial and military opinion highly comforting to enemies of the United States.

By contrast, in this struggle, lawyers who oppose either the government's goals or its methods or both have taken to the courts in an effort not only to blunt the weapons employed by the executive branch but also to overwhelm and prevail by sheer volume of litigation. One prominent practitioner of the self-congratulatory activity known as public interest advocacy has said frankly, and accurately, that there are thousands of lawyers ready and willing to overwhelm the federal courts with litigation on behalf of detainees, if only given the chance. And the courts have opened their doors to the effort. Explaining why that has happened would take many pages. But the willingness of the courts to step in where the legislative branch has abdicated means that the outcome of a deadly struggle is as likely to turn on who has more or better lawyers as on who has stronger forces.

Previous wars presented a far more straightforward path to victory than the war on terrorism. In World War II, for example, the enemy was clearly defined. So was our objective: to smash the enemy's war-making machinery and, if necessary, some of its civilian infrastructure and compel a formal surrender. All of this could be accomplished with conventional armed forces fighting other conventional armed forces. Islamic terrorists do not present this tidy target. They do not occupy a particular geographic location and indeed hide among civilian populations. One of our most critical assets is intelligence. Unless we can find out who is planning what, there is nothing to do but await attack and rely either on good fortune or heroism to stop it, or on first responders to mitigate its effects.

There are essentially two ways to gather intelligence. One relies on technology – electronic intercepts of various kinds. The other relies on people. The former requires that we try to listen in on those planning to attack us; the latter requires that we elicit from those who directly participate in those plans the people who participated, what they plan to do, and how. The two are sometimes referred to with the shorthand "signals intelligence" and "human intelligence." When we investigate conventional criminal conspiracies like drug gangs, it is sometimes possible to insinuate an informant or undercover agent into the ranks of the conspirators and thereby monitor and eventually thwart the conspiracy. Terrorist organizations vet their operatives carefully. Also, we have few operatives, if any, capable of passing as native speakers of Arabic or Pashtu or Urdu, or as convincing members of those cultures. In any event, infiltration entails

---

Unless we can find out who is planning what, there is nothing to do but await attack and rely either on good fortune or heroism to stop it, or on first responders to mitigate its effects.

---

much time and high risk and yields only spotty results. That leaves questioning of captured terrorists as a necessary and important way to gather reliable human intelligence.

Why gather human intelligence at all? Isn't signals intelligence, captured in real time from the actual malefactors, far more reliable than information from human beings, who may be motivated to lie or may err even in the best of faith? Well . . . no. One veteran intelligence hand has analogized the process of gathering and weighing intelligence to trying to put together a huge jigsaw puzzle without looking at the picture on the box. Occasionally, he notes, a human being who has actually seen the picture, or a part of it, comes to hand, and it then becomes vital to get as many details of that picture as possible.

Those charged with gathering intelligence in the wake of the September 11 attacks understood that. They relied on Congress's Authorization for Use of Military Force to justify gathering signals intelligence even under circumstances that might violate then-existing statutes and standards under the Fourth Amendment clause barring unreasonable searches and seizures. They argued that one of the functions of the military in times of war was to gather intelligence, and any such intelligence gathering was, by definition, reasonable. As memories of the September 11 attacks faded, safety begat complacency, and this reading of the congressional resolution came to be seen by many as overly aggressive. What became known as the Terrorist Surveillance Program was the subject of a bitter tug-of-war between President Bush and Congress, last resolved in 2008, when that program was folded into existing law and portions placed under the scrutiny of the Foreign Intelligence Surveillance Court.

The struggle over the gathering of human intelligence was another matter. In March 2002, an al Qaeda operative named Abu Zubaydah came into the hands of the CIA following his capture by Pakistani agents. He was seriously wounded and was believed to be in possession of essential information about al

Qaeda. He was treated for his wounds in the custody of the CIA by the finest medical talent available in the United States. While still recovering from his wounds and dependent on his interrogators for comfort, he gave up some information voluntarily. He inadvertently disclosed the alias ("Mukhtar") of Khalid Sheikh Mohammed (KSM), the mastermind of the September 11 attacks. But having been essentially the travel agent for al Qaeda operatives all over the world and one of only a few people who had direct contact with the top level of al Qaeda, Abu Zubaydah was believed to harbor much more valuable information. His initial questioning was led by the FBI, but as he grew both physically and psychologically stronger and less communicative, he was turned over to the CIA.

That agency devised a regimen of techniques for inducing cooperation during interrogation, later to become known by the Orwellian euphemism "enhanced interrogation techniques." Using the word "enhanced" could not have been more unfortunate. Such an anodyne term, more suggestive of a washday detergent or a suntan lotion than a method of breaking a person's will, looked like a disingenuous verbal flinch, an attempt to fool the listener into excusing the inexcusable. The techniques were rough stuff, including firm but openhanded slaps to the side of the face or the abdomen; banging the subject's shoulders against a specially constructed wall that exaggerated with sound the apparent force involved; sleep deprivation; and ultimately waterboarding – a technique, which will be discussed further, that induced in the subject the panic that accompanies drowning.

The CIA, mindful of the domestic statutory bar on torture, submitted the proposed techniques, which included one or two not mentioned above, to the Justice Department. It included a precise description not only of the techniques themselves, but also of the precise manner and the limitations and safeguards, including medical safeguards, with which they were to be administered to a population that would necessarily select itself based on resistance to less coercive measures. Further, such techniques were to be administered only by people specially trained in them, only to people believed to have vital actionable intelligence, and only with the direct approval of senior CIA leadership. In detailed but hurriedly prepared memos, the Justice Department approved as lawful most, but not all, of the proposed techniques. These hurriedly prepared memos eventually were withdrawn, and others were substituted in 2005 as more soundly reasoned. But the conclusions remained the same. The techniques in question did not violate the torture statute.

These memoranda would come to be known collectively in the popular media as the "torture memos," notwithstanding that they were drafted with the intention of avoiding any technique that constituted torture while marking out the limits of what the law allows. For all of the controversy over the memos and the interrogation program pursued by the CIA, of the many thousands of terrorists captured by U.S. forces, fewer than 1,000 were detained in the CIA's so-called "black sites"; of those, fewer than a third were subject to any of the harsh interrogation techniques discussed in the memos; and of those, three – Abu Zubaydah; Khalid Sheikh Mohammed; and Abd al-Rahim al-Nashiri, the mastermind of the USS *Cole* bombing – were waterboarded. According to those in a position to know, all three provided actionable intelligence following their exposure to these methods.

Notably, Zubaydah, according to both George Tenet and Gen. Michael Hayden, former CIA directors, provided information that led to the capture of Ramzi bin al-Shibh. In addition to having been the principal communications link between the 9/11 hijackers in the United States and al Qaeda leadership abroad, al-Shibh was arrested while he was completing plans to stage another 9/11-style attack on the Canary Wharf business district in London and Heathrow Airport. Intelligence officials had known nothing of these plans before the arrest. In addition, he provided information that led to the arrest in Chicago of Jose Padilla, an American-born jihadi who, after he served time for manslaughter in this country, undertook a journey of personal discovery that led to an introduction to KSM and other al Qaeda luminaries. Padilla was known principally for what seems to have been a fanciful plot to build and detonate a "dirty bomb" – a device that yields a small explosion but a high level of radiation. Far more serious, and unprosecuted because the necessary evidence could not be presented in a federal court, was his plan with an accomplice to acquire apartments in Florida, seal them, fill them with natural gas, and detonate them simultaneously to cause widespread civilian death and destruction. He was convicted of lesser charges of aiding overseas terrorist activities but nonetheless received a lengthy sentence.

Zubaydah also revealed that he and others in al Qaeda had been trained to resist interrogation but were also taught that they were permitted by Allah to disclose information when they reached the limit of their ability to withstand physical and psychological pressure. This in itself was invaluable intelligence. Moreover, a later claim by FBI agent Ali Soufan, that the information about Padilla had been obtained by his establishing rapport with Zubaydah, was belied by Soufan's own partner and a report by the Justice Department's inspector general into interrogation procedures.

When the lessons learned from the questioning of Zubaydah were applied to KSM, including the lesson about reaching the limits of resistance, the result was an intelligence bonanza. KSM became the tutor to his captors and disclosed both general information on how al Qaeda moved money and people and specific information that led to the interruption of other plots. These included yet another plot involving airplanes, aimed at the Library Tower in Los Angeles, to be carried out by members of a South Asian terrorist affiliate called Jemaah Islamiyah, led by a man named Hambali. When further information was received as the result of leads from KSM, he was questioned yet again and disclosed a key telephone number that identified a circle of terrorist plotters. Still further information from KSM identified an al Qaeda program to develop a biological weapons capability in the United States that included the production of anthrax, and the capture of people involved in that program led to yet further intelligence.

Al-Nashiri, the USS *Cole* mastermind, provided out-of-date information when first questioned. But after he was subjected to harsh interrogation techniques, including waterboarding, he provided important information about al Qaeda's current operational planning.

It is important to note both how these techniques and the actual questioning interacted, and how intelligence is used. These techniques were not applied by those who conduct questioning and debriefings, but by operators or interrogators specially trained to apply them. Each was applied not alone but in tandem with other techniques in a regimen that had to be approved in advance by senior CIA personnel, and then only after a detainee had been noncompliant. Still further restrictions applied to waterboarding. Once the detainee indicated that he was ready to be compliant, a debriefer resumed questioning. So it is not possible to say with certainty that this or that particular technique yielded this or that particular item of information, only that after these three detainees were subjected to techniques that included waterboarding, they provided actionable intelligence when they had refused to do so before and that others subjected to some subset of other techniques did likewise.

There is no substance to the claim that these techniques are not productive because a detainee would do anything to stop the discomfort, including lie. If the object were to elicit confessions, the claim might be valid. Subject anyone to enough waterboarding, and he might confess to having shot Abraham Lincoln. But the object is not confessions; it is intelligence. Facts disclosed by detainees under interrogation are not taken at face value. They are fit into the matrix of other facts known to intelligence officers in order to test their reliability.

In any event, with both mounting criticism of coercive techniques and increasing knowledge about al Qaeda that could be used to interrogate captured operatives, waterboarding was abandoned as a part of the CIA interrogation program in 2003. It could not, under rules applied during the Bush administration, be restored to the program absent a specific request from the director of the CIA and the approval of both the president and the attorney general. The CIA interrogation program as a whole, however, including waterboarding, remained classified. In the seven-plus years following September 11, 2001, although several plots aimed at us had been broken up, both within the country and outside it, there had been no successful terrorist attacks within the United States.

In his inaugural address on January 20, 2009, President Obama announced, "As for our common defense, we reject as false the choice between our safety and our ideals." Two days later, at a White House ceremony, he promised to return America to the "moral high ground" in the struggle against terrorism. He signed three executive orders. One directed that the military detention facility at Guantanamo be closed within a year. A second order said that no one being held in the

---

In the seven-plus years following September 11, 2001, although several plots aimed at us had been broken up, there had been no successful terrorist attacks within the United States.

---

custody of any government department or agency in any armed conflict could be interrogated using any technique other than one authorized in the Army Field Manual. The third halted all military commission proceedings pending further review and also effectively halted a Supreme Court appeal by Ali Saleh Kahlah al-Marri, who, by his own admission, came to the United States on direct order of KSM to help organize a second wave of attacks following the September 11, 2001, atrocity and was the only person then held in the mainland United States as an unlawful enemy combatant.

The closing of Guantanamo, Obama said, would "restore the standards of due process and the core constitutional values that have made this country great even in the midst of war, even in dealing with terrorism." Restricting interrogators to the Army Field Manual "reflects the best judgment of our military that we can abide by a rule that says we don't torture but that we can still effectively obtain the intelligence that we need." All in all, he said, the orders reflected "me following through ... on an understanding that dates back to our founding fathers, that we are willing to observe core standards of conduct not just when it's easy but also when it's hard."

Guantanamo is a military, not CIA, installation. When it was first set up to house unlawful combatants captured abroad, it was primitive and became the focus of invective, most of it ill-informed, about prisoner abuse. This was particularly true in the aftermath of the Abu Ghraib incident in Iraq, in which prisoners were tormented and humiliated simply for the amusement of undisciplined soldiers. Guantanamo was upgraded at great cost when it became clear that we needed a place to house unlawful combatants and try those who could be charged with war crimes.

I visited Guantanamo in February 2008, while serving as attorney general, and had occasion when I was a district judge to visit federal detention facilities in the United States. Guantanamo is a state-of-the-art facility that compares favorably with even medium-security federal prisons in this country. Because it is remote and located on an island, there is less need for the restrictive conditions that prevail at maximum-security facilities here. I saw where the most noted detainees are housed and would have seen KSM himself had he not been meeting that day with representatives of the International Committee of the Red Cross. In his absence, I was able to visit his cell and adjoining exercise area, which featured the same make and model of elliptical machine that I used in the gym at the building where I lived in Washington, D.C., although of course I, unlike KSM, had to share the machine with others. Detainees may choose from a menu of nutritionally balanced halal meals (my lunch came from that menu), and they are provided with a copy of the Koran in a bag to assure them that it was not touched by infidels. The base itself includes new courtrooms in which to try military commission cases, with secure electronic communications and storage equipment that can handle information at any level of classification from anywhere in the world. It has a gallery for press and other observers that can be electronically screened off when classified information is being presented but otherwise has a full view of the proceedings accompanied by simultaneous translation. This trial facility was built at a cost of tens of millions of dollars and is unequaled at any courthouse in the United States.

That is not to say that there isn't violence at Guantanamo. There is plenty of it, but it is directed by the prisoners toward the guards, not the other way. I saw the plastic face shields that guards must wear when they approach or enter cells to protect them from the cocktails of urine, feces, and semen that are regularly hurled at them along with verbal and physical abuse. I saw the collection of weapons fashioned by detainees to attack guards, as well as the rigorous standards imposed on the guards in responding to these provocations. Any lapse of behavior or demeanor by a military guard results in swift discipline or transfer. Prisoners receive better medical care at Guantanamo than their captors. Notwithstanding prisoners' access to a substantial library of Arabic videos, the most frequently viewed were episodes of *Walker, Texas Ranger*. Despite the abuse these guards take and the thankless rigor of their day-to-day existence,

I received only one request from any of them: Please tell people what this place is really like.

The Army Field Manual, to which the president confined interrogators in one of his January 22, 2009, orders, was written to set limits for battlefield interrogations that could be carried out by young recruits. The limits of that manual were not set with experienced and closely supervised interrogators in mind. The manual itself has long been available on the Internet, and has, in fact, been used to help train al Qaeda operatives, who now know precisely what they face not only from soldiers in the field, but from any U.S. captor.

The president's new secretary of the Department of Homeland Security, Janet Napolitano, shuns the terms "terrorism" and "war," as does the president, preferring to describe the former as "man-caused disasters" and the latter as "foreign contingency operations." When she first assumed office, she was unaware that it was a crime for an alien to enter this country unlawfully and thought the 9/11 plotters came to this country from Canada.

For his attorney general, the president chose Eric Holder, a man who said during the 2008 campaign that the government had "authorized the use of torture, approved of secret electronic surveillance against American citizens, secretly detained American citizens without due process of law, denied the writ of habeas corpus to hundreds of accused enemy combatants, and authorized the use of procedures that violate both international law and the United States Constitution." He added, "We owe the American people a reckoning." During his confirmation hearing, although he had not been briefed on details of classified CIA interrogation practices, he stated flatly that waterboarding is torture, a position with which he found no conflict even when it was pointed out to him at a later hearing that Navy SEALs and other special forces are waterboarded routinely as part of their training. Training was not torture, he said, because the intent was different, although he continued to maintain that waterboarding in other settings, apparently regardless of how it was administered or with what purpose, was torture, notwithstanding that the one and only relevant statute that defines torture states that it is an act committed under color of law and "specifically intended to inflict severe physical or mental pain or suffering." Asked during an appearance in Berlin whether he would cooperate with foreign or international courts trying to prosecute former Bush administration officials for engaging in torture, he responded: "This is an administration that is determined to conduct itself by the rule of law. And to the extent that we receive lawful requests from an appropriately created court, we would obviously respond to it."

In April 2009, what seemed to be the promised "reckoning" would begin with the release of the theretofore classified Department of Justice memoranda analyzing the legality of the CIA's interrogation procedures adopted in the aftermath of 9/11, which included a detailed description of the procedures and limits of each technique. That disclosure, made in the name of openness, was transparently intended to stir a wind of outrage that would drive further "reckoning."

As to waterboarding, the memos disclosed that it involved binding a detainee to a tilted bench, head downward, covering his nose and mouth with a cloth, and pouring water on the cloth, with the result that airflow is restricted for 20 to 40 seconds, causing a resulting increase in the carbon dioxide level in the blood and an automatically increased effort to breathe. The presence of the cloth inhibiting breathing and the increased carbon dioxide level created in the detainee a reflexive feeling of "suffocation and incipient panic," even if the detainee was aware he was not going to drown, as he would be after an initial application. If a detainee tried to defeat the technique, for example by holding his breath or turning his head to the side, the operator could wait until the detainee started to breathe before applying water, or cup his hands around the detainee's nose and mouth to dam the runoff and prevent breathing. This procedure was applied only with a physician present and monitoring a detainee's physical condition; it caused virtually no physical pain and caused no lasting psychological damage. In addition, it could be authorized only if the CIA had credible information that a terrorist attack was imminent, that the subject had actionable intelligence with respect to it, and that other techniques had failed or were unlikely to yield timely actionable intelligence.

Disclosure of these memos did not elicit the outrage that was anticipated. Rather, it was obvious that the CIA, with the concurrence of the Justice Department, had taken extraordinary care to avoid inflicting torture. It became obvious as well that the equation drawn by politicians and pundits linking the CIA procedure and the practices of the Japanese during World War II or the Khmer Rouge in Cambodia was absurd. Those practices included forcing water down a prisoner's throat until his innards were painfully swollen, then stepping on his stomach to force the water out, or submerging a prisoner's head in a tank of water while he was handcuffed to the bottom until he either nearly or actually drowned. Although both were called "waterboarding," the CIA procedure bore as little resemblance to the cruelty of the Japanese or the Khmer Rouge as an arduous hike did to the Bataan Death March. What certainly was achieved by these disclosures, however, was broadcasting to our enemies the precise legal limits to which any president could press them, thus permitting them to train for the absolute worst.

Hard on the heels of disclosure of the memoranda came more "reckoning" – the attorney general's appointment of a prosecutor to reconsider whether criminal charges should be brought against CIA interrogators in cases that had already been reviewed by career prosecutors and deemed insufficient to warrant prosecution. Although those prosecutors prepared detailed memoranda describing the facts and the legal reasons for their conclusions, the attorney general conceded, astoundingly, that he had not read those memoranda before directing the reopening of those cases.

In early June, Ahmed Ghailani, confined at

Guantanamo for numerous war crimes that could have been tried before a military tribunal, would be brought instead to New York to face already pending civilian charges in connection with the 1998 bombing of U.S. embassies in East Africa. After experiencing confinement in a civilian jail, Ghailani has asked to be returned to Guantanamo to await his trial, a preview of what is to come if Guantanamo detainees are brought here.

November and December 2009 brought additional examples of the current administration's approach to Islamic terrorism. The first came in November, at Fort Hood, Texas. Nidal Malik Hasan was an Army psychiatrist who held the rank of major and had a history of anti-American and pro-jihadi statements even while he treated soldiers returning from combat at Walter Reed Army Medical Center in Washington, D.C. He had been detected to be in communication with a fanatic Muslim cleric named Anwar al-Awlaki, also an American, who had preached to at least two of the 9/11 hijackers while they were in this country.

Hasan shouted "allahu akbar" – Allah is great – before opening fire on waiting patients in Fort Hood's Soldier Readiness Center, killing 13 and wounding about 30. The president warned the country against jumping to conclusions about the nature and motive of the act.

Also in November, Attorney General Holder announced that he had decided to terminate military commission proceedings against KSM and others charged with planning the 9/11 attacks, as those proceedings were about to start and KSM had already declared his intention to plead guilty. Instead, KSM and the others would be brought to New York to be charged and stand trial in a civilian proceeding in federal court in Manhattan, blocks from where the World Trade Center stood. This, he said, would show the world that we were committed to upholding the rule of law. He did not specify which law, although it certainly could not be the law that permitted unlawful combatants, or unprivileged enemy belligerents, as they are now called, to be tried before military commissions. Nor did he explain how treating those who violate the Geneva Conventions and other laws better than those who obey them would promote the rule of law. A chorus of criticism, arising from the obvious threat and disruption to New York City that would result from such a trial and the cost of protecting against it, has resulted in reconsideration of where that trial will be held. But it is by no means clear that the obvious alternative of continuing the military commission proceeding in Guantanamo even will be considered.

On Christmas Day 2009, in an airplane over Detroit, Umar Farouk Abdulmutallab, a Nigerian terrorist trained by al Qaeda in Yemen, allegedly tried to ignite a bomb secreted in his undershorts that would have killed 289 passengers and crew, plus untold others on the ground. He was seated in the particular seat on the airplane where an explosion would have caused the maximum damage. His apparent lack of manual dexterity, combined with the heroic intervention of passengers and crew after he had gotten as far as starting a fire, prevented the explosion. His father had warned State Department officials that he had become radicalized; electronic intercepts months before had warned of an incipient plot involving a Nigerian; he bought his ticket for cash and carried no luggage. Yet withal, he was allowed to board the airplane. Further, after he landed and was willingly disclosing information of substantial intelligence value to FBI agents, the attorney general directed that civilian rather than military processes be employed and that he be warned of his *Miranda* rights to silence and counsel. Upon the advice of his lawyer, Abdulmutallab provided no further information. A day after the incident, the secretary of the Department of Homeland Security pronounced that the system had worked, and a day after that was ready to say that there was no larger terrorist plot. The director of national intelligence, after testifying that if consulted, he would have sent Abdulmutallab to a special interrogation group put in place to question high-value detainees, conceded that that group was devised to deal only with detainees apprehended abroad, and in any event did not yet exist. As of this writing, Abdulmutallab's family, flown here from Nigeria, convinced him to continue his disclosures some five weeks after he stopped. What sort of arrangement has been offered him in return is not yet clear. Abdulmutallab has been indicted in Detroit and apparently is to be prosecuted in a civilian court. Curiously, that indictment did not initially contain a conspiracy charge, which would tend to show that his initial disclosures, at least, did not contain enough information to charge anyone else.

What was known, for all its shortcomings of nomenclature, as the global war on terrorism appears to have fallen victim to a mindset in which the pure and the lofty trump reality. All we have to do, the president said in his inaugural address, is to choose hope over fear, reject as false the choice between our safety and our ideals, and we can have it all – yes we can. If we strike the right pose, the world will applaud. So it is thought to be of no real significance that both the president and his chief law enforcement officer call for a civilian trial that will showcase the fairness of our legal system, even as they guarantee, when righteous indignation seems more to the taste of the gallery, that the outcome of that trial will

---

The global war on terrorism appears to have fallen victim to a mindset in which the pure and the lofty trump reality.

---

be conviction and the death penalty. Nor does it matter that in treating unlawful combatants more favorably than lawful ones, we undo more than a century of effort to civilize the rules of warfare, and we undermine our own safety in the process. A world like that, where choices have no consequences, is a world inhabited only by children, and then only in their fantasies. If we try to live in it, we do so at peril to ourselves and our children.

First American edition published in 2010 by Encounter Books, an activity of Encounter for Culture and Education, Inc., a nonprofit, tax exempt corporation.
Encounter Books website address: www.encounterbooks.com

Manufactured in the United States and printed on acid-free paper. The paper used in this publication meets the minimum requirements of ANSI/NISO Z39.48–1992 (R 1997) (*Permanence of Paper*).

LIBRARY OF CONGRESS CATALOGING-IN-PUBLICATION DATA

Mukasey, Michael Bernard, 1941–
How Obama has mishandled the War on Terror / by Michael Mukasey.
p. cm. — (Encounter broadsides)
ISBN-13: 978-1-59403-489-3 (pbk. : alk. paper)
ISBN-10: 1-59403-489-3 (pbk. : alk. paper)
1. War on Terrorism, 2001–2009. 2. United States—Foreign relations—2009– 3. Obama, Barack. I. Title.
HV6432.M847 2010
973.932092—dc22
2010005337

10 9 8 7 6 5 4 3 2 1

SERIES DESIGN BY CARL W. SCARBROUGH